Prayer

*Where to start &
how to keep going*

Stephen Cottrell

CHURCH HOUSE
PUBLISHING

Published 2020 by Church House Publishing

www.chpublishing.co.uk

Church House Publishing, Church House,
Great Smith Street, London SW1P 3AZ

Much of the material contained here is adapted from *Praying Through Life* and *How to Pray*, which are © Stephen Cottrell 1998, 2003, 2010

ISBN 978 1 78140 214 6

A catalogue record for this book is available from the British Library

Designed and illustrated by www.penguinboy.net

Printed in the UK by Ashford Colour Press Ltd

Contents

Introduction

This little booklet aims to help you start praying.

It is adapted from a larger book that was first called **Praying through Life** and then re-published as **How to Pray**. It is about praying on your own, with others when you can, and at any time and in any place.

It still feels a little presumptuous to write on this subject. I don't claim any great expertise. But I do hope that a muddled beginner like me might actually be the best sort of person to write this sort of book, since there is little danger that I will ever get very far ahead of those I'm trying to lead.

There is no right way of praying. There are just the ways that are right for you. But there is also the great heritage of praying that we can learn from and explore.

My prayer for this booklet is to simply get you started and then help you keep going in the dogged, delightful, painful and puzzling business of daily prayer; of weaving prayer into daily life; of living life with God; to make it seem possible; and to be realistic about its joys and challenges.

This little booklet can help you build a prayer life at home: one that can sustain you during times of isolation and beyond.

Stephen Cottrell

June 2020

Question 1

What is prayer and how do I start?

So, what's the secret of prayer? The American monk and activist Thomas Merton once wrote: "The secret of prayer is hunger for God. The will to pray is the essence of prayer."

I don't feel I've ever got much beyond this.

Most of my prayer seems to be taking up with my longing for God and my longing to pray. Most books I've read about prayer don't tell you this. They tend to describe the benefits of prayer, but gloss over the mechanics of getting there.

Here you will find some practical advice and encouragement to actually start praying.

The hardest thing about prayer is beginning. So just start.

Your wanting to pray is the beginning of a relationship with God that can grow and grow. And it can start anywhere.

Don't worry if you find it difficult. It doesn't depend on you nearly as much as you think. "I cannot pray," the great Dutch spiritual writer Henri Nouwen once said, "but God can pray in me." It took me a long while to learn this, and even so it is a truth I often forget. I imagine prayer to be somehow dependent on my effort, or worse, my eloquence.

God calls out to every human heart and longs to make a home in every human heart. But God waits for us to respond.

There is a paradox to prayer. It is all about the gift of God, and God praying in us, but it also has to be an act of human will. God calls out to every human heart and longs to make a home in every human heart. But God waits for us to respond. When we do, it is God's delight to come to us and sing his song within us. Our voice - however faint and unsure of the tune - is joined to the song of the Spirit.

Question 1

My own working definition of prayer is this: Prayer is the lover coming into the presence of the beloved and saying, "I love you."

This is an entirely different way of thinking about prayer. It is not about what we "put in" or "get out", but focuses entirely on God.

God is the great lover. We are God's beloved. God is constantly coming into our presence to say that he loves us. Most of the time, we probably won't be aware of this. But that doesn't mean God isn't there. We aren't usually aware of the air we breathe. But we keep on breathing.

Prayer is the most natural thing in the world. It has been said that prayer is as natural as a flower opening its petals to the sun.

But it can also be the hardest.

There will be dark and difficult times when prayer feels impossible. It requires discipline as well as desire. Because it is relationship, it is about letting go and allowing someone else to be at the centre of your life.

I am not a Christian because I know lots of things *about* God, but because I *know* God. This relationship, which God has initiated through his love, is one we enter freely. God will never force his way into our lives. But the great paradox of this relationship is that when we put Jesus at the centre of our life, he puts us at the centre of his.

Like all relationships, it needs to be worked at. And it is through prayer that our relationship with God is nurtured and sustained.

"You learn to pray by praying."

ELIZABETH OBBARD,
TO LIVE IS TO PRAY

There is no right way, or place or posture for praying. Just the way that is right for you. Feeling comfortable is vital. You don't, for instance, have to kneel down. Sitting in an easy chair, or lying on the floor is just as good.

Using set prayers is one of the best ways to get started. If you use your own words, do not worry that they won't be good enough. Even if you find you find you have no words, offer God your thoughts, even your distractions and anxieties. Give him the time you have set aside.

Almighty God, to whom all hearts are open,
all desires known,
and from whom no secrets are hidden:
cleanse the thoughts of our hearts
by the inspiration of your Holy Spirit,
that we may perfectly love you,
and worthily magnify your holy name;
through Christ our Lord. Amen.

A PRAYER OF PREPARATION (THE COLLECT FOR PURITY)
FROM COMMON WORSHIP

Question 2

Where and when should I pray?

Some people say prayer is like eating. We don't eat all the time, but we need regular meals to resource us for everything else that happens during the day. Think of those times that you set aside for prayer as your chance to sit down and eat with God and receive what you need for the rest of the day.

Some people say it is like breathing. Something we do all the time.

"Pray all the time,"
says St Paul.

"Pray all the time," says St Paul (1 Thessalonians 5.17).
I don't think he means do that activity we call "prayer" all the time. I think he means make your life a prayer. But to do that, we probably need focused moments of prayer. Over time - like a fine wine maturing in the barrel, or an onion being pickled in vinegar - we are slowly changed. We become prayerful.

"A love letter from God"

The whole Christian story of the birth, life, teaching, death and resurrection of Jesus Christ could be summed up as a "love letter from God".

In Jesus, God declares his love for us. What we call prayer, those stumbling, faltering words that we use to speak to God, is simply our response.

In other words, prayer can become like breathing. And it needs to be regular like eating. But it is most like loving. And it is most like loving because it is, at heart, a relationship.

This is the most basic truth about prayer. Prayer is relationship with God; it is the relationship we are made for. Like all relationships it is not easy to describe. I know what it feels like to be in love. But it is hard to define it. Put together all the most beautiful love poems in the world and they are as nothing compared with a few moments of love itself.

Being a Christian is like a love affair. In Jesus we see how God gives himself to us in love. "As the Father has loved me," says Jesus, "so I have loved you." (John 15.9)

Prayer is an act of love and a participation in the life of love. In Jesus, God declares his love for us. In prayer we come into communion with God to express our love to him.

So prayer can happen everywhere and anywhere. It's not just something that happens in a church or other special place. Neither does it depend on special times – although we probably still need those special times to nurture the relationship.

So prayer can happen everywhere and anywhere. It's not just something that happens in a church or other special place.

"The whole reason why we pray is summed up in the sight and vision of him to whom we pray ... the more the soul sees God, the more by his grace does it want him."

MOTHER JULIAN OF NORWICH

What images or objects remind you that God is there? Think about how you could make a special place for prayer at home. When you're on the go, you might try carrying something in your pocket or handbag, or putting an image on your phone's lock screen.

Could you set yourself an alarm to remind yourself it's time to pray? Think about when you could take a couple of moments in your busy day to check in with God.

Merciful God,
you have prepared for those who love you
such good things as pass our understanding:
pour into our hearts such love toward you
that we, loving you in all things
and above all things,
may obtain your promises,
which exceed all that we can desire;
through Jesus our Lord. Amen.

THE COLLECT FOR THE SIXTH SUNDAY AFTER TRINITY,
COMMON WORSHIP

Question 3

How should I pray?

When you were at school you were probably taught to put your hands together when you prayed. But in one of his many books about prayer, Henri Nouwen says that when we pray "we are asked to open up our tightly clenched fists".

So why not start by holding your clenched fist in front of you, and then slowly opening it up to receive from God the blessings and wisdom God longs to give you.

In this way – your hands open before God – your hand itself can be a basic pattern and reminder of how to pray.

Using your hand as a model for prayer

1. Thumb

When something is good you give it the "thumbs up". So start with thanksgiving. Count your blessings. What are the good things in your life? Thank God for them.

2. Index finger

This is the finger you use to point. Pray for direction in your life; the decisions you need to make; the things for which you are responsible; the things you are concerned about. Pray for direction in our world and for the challenges we face.

3. Middle finger

This is the tallest finger. Pray for the important people who have power in the world; national and local politicians; the Royal Family and other world leaders and their governments.

4. Ring finger

If you are married, you wear your wedding ring on this finger. It is also the weakest finger. It can't do much on its own. Pray for your family and friends. Pray for the people upon whom you are dependent, and the people who are dependent on you.

5. Little finger

This is the smallest and the last finger on your hand. Pray for the poor, the weak, the helpless, the vulnerable, the excluded, the hungry, the sick, the ill and the bereaved. Remember those who have died.

And finally – lifting both your hands to God in thanksgiving – pray for yourself.

The sign of the cross

This leads us to probably one of the most basic ways of praying of all, also using your hands. Making a sign of the cross on your forehead or your body. It is one of the ways many Christians begin and end a time of prayer.

The sign of the cross reminds us that we belong to Jesus.

In Baptism – the start of the Christian life – we are marked with the sign of the cross, the sign that we are saved by the suffering and death of Christ. In death – if we receive the last rites – we are marked with the cross again. The sign of the cross reminds us that we belong to Jesus, the crucified one.

"*Prayer is not an activity of the mind, for God is not in the head. It is an activity of the whole person, and God is in the wholeness.*"

KEN LEECH, *SOUL FRIEND*

What do you think of when you make the sign of the cross? Many Christians think of the Father, the Son, and the Holy Spirit. Is there a verse from the Bible or a short prayer that you find helpful to call to mind?

Try listing the things you are thankful for in the morning when you get up. Does this sometimes lead you into prayer?

God be in my head,
and in my understanding;
God be in my eyes,
and in my looking;
God be in my mouth,
and in my speaking;
God be in my heart,
and in my thinking;
God be at mine end,
and at my departing.

SARUM PRIMER

Question 4

How do I build prayer into everyday life?

Most of us have routines that shape the day. One of the ways of developing a life of prayer is to weave times of prayer into these existing rhythms and routines. If we attend to some simple spiritual disciplines and rhythms to shape our day, we are also more likely to maintain good mental health.

Each point in the day lends itself to a different sort of praying:

First thing in the morning

When you get up in the morning and clean your teeth. Or when you jump in the shower. Or when you open the curtains for the first time - use this as an opportunity to welcome the new day. Dedicate the day to God, asking that you will receive the sustenance you need.

This kind of prayer is sometimes called a consecration of the day to God.

At mealtimes

Eating is still one of the main routines that shape a day.

When you sit down to eat, say a prayer of thanksgiving for your food. This is a very basic sort of prayer. It enables us not just to give thanks for the food in front of us, but for all those whose lives are connected with ours, and for all the ways God provides for us.

I might want to give thanks for those who plant and grow and pick and transport and stack and sell the food that ends up on my plate.

This kind of prayer is called thanksgiving. It is primarily for the food and those whose labour has provided it. But it can also be a brief opportunity to give thanks to God for all the things that sustain life, not least God's own unending grace and goodness.

It's worth remembering that the word Eucharist (one of the names Christians have for Holy Communion) means thanksgiving. The most basic act of worship in the church is a meal. And it is a thank you meal.

As you exercise

When you take your daily walk (or run or cycle) you are likely to be on your own. Why not use this as an opportunity to pray for others as well as yourself. Perhaps list in your mind the people you are concerned about and the other things that are closest to your heart.

This kind of prayer is usually called intercession. It is that prayer when we bring to God the people and things that are on our hearts.

At the end of the day

At the end of the day you could say the ancient office of Night Prayer (or Compline). This is a service of quiet reflection for the end of the day, deriving its name from the Latin word meaning completion.

It includes an opportunity to think over the day, what is sometimes called an examination of conscience. We bring to God what has happened in the day. The things that have gone well and the things that have gone wrong. The things we should have said and done as well as the wrong things we ended up saying and doing.

This kind of prayer is called confession. We acknowledge our need of God, our sinfulness, and we cry out for God's abundant mercy and goodness.

We also finish the day as we started: thanking God for the blessings of the day; and praying for rest and safety through the night.

―――――――――

Not all these things will work for everyone. Some things that work one day, won't work so well the next. Find the way of praying that is right for you, and then build on it, trying other new things from time to time. And perhaps speak to friends about how it is going and what works for them.

"Love to pray.
Feel often during the day
the need for prayer, and
take trouble to pray.
If you want to pray better,
you must pray more."

MOTHER TERESA OF CALCUTTA,
IN THE SILENCE OF THE HEART

Think about the rhythms and routines of your daily life. Make time for God by discerning where in each day are your times and places for prayer.

Try giving thanks before a meal – with others or on your own. Keep it short and simple, such as "O Lord, bless this food to our use and us in your service, and keep us ever mindful of the needs of others. Amen."

Time to Pray from the Church of England offers a simple service of Prayer During the Day and Night Prayer you could use as your basic diet of daily prayer. There's a free app with audio, a booklet, and you can also follow it online: **CofE.io/TimetoPray**

Save us, O Lord, while waking,
and guard us while sleeping,
that awake we may watch with Christ
and asleep may rest in peace. Amen.

COMMON WORSHIP NIGHT PRAYER

Question 5

How do I pray with my family?

The question I'm going to explore here isn't, of course, relevant to everyone – though it will be a very important one for some. And many of the principles below can – and, perhaps, should – apply to how we pray as adults, too.

In my experience, children love to pray. Their ease with God spans Christian traditions. They thrive on routine and will be in enthralled by the comfort and the colour of ritual. They love the Word of God and will listen over and over again to stories from the Bible. Their prayer will be spontaneous, joyful and creative.

When I first started to explore ways of praying together at home with small children, I looked around for the books on the subject. I couldn't find any. There are plenty of books of prayer for children, but nothing much about how to pray with children.

Here are a few ideas for praying with children and with teenagers and as a whole family.

With children

With younger children it is important to understand how they develop and particularly the importance of routine. When our own children were small, we tried to make prayer a natural part of the day the rhythm of life. Tea time, bath time, story time and prayer time all followed each other in a comfortingly familiar daily routine.

That prayer included daily rituals of sitting down together, lighting a candle and saying a set prayer. But it also included spontaneity and creativity. Using pictures the children had made themselves as a focus of the prayer, allowing them to give expression to their prayer. And making sure that the whole thing was punctuated by stories from the Bible.

Small children learn through play. It is the way they come to understand the world around them … we must make praying like playing.

Small children learn through play. It is the way they come to understand the world around them. They reproduce the world through their play, solving problems and re-enacting its dramas and delights. So, we must make praying like playing.

Whenever we pray in the home with children, teenagers or as a couple, or even on our own, we need to try and weave together these three elements.

Ritual – using familiar prayers and secure patterns of prayer and developing our own little family rituals of prayer.

Spontaneity – nurturing within ourselves and in our households ways of expressing prayer in response to what has happened to us in the day. Both thanksgiving and petition.

Play – praying should be fun!

Some years ago, a Sunday school teacher asked me if I had noticed that adults' prayers usually began with the word "please", but children's prayers always began with the words "thank you".

It is a most challenging observation. When we adults come to God, it tends to be with all the stuff we want to ask God to do for us. But children come with thanksgiving on their lips.

So when we pray with children, it is not us praying for them, but us praying with them, and asking them to lead us in prayer. Often where we may dither and hesitate, their praying gets right to the heart of a situation in ways we find embarrassing or difficult.

With teenagers

Praying with teenagers will always be more challenging. Probably the most important lesson to learn is not to force them or expect them to join in if they don't want to. Teenagers are very interested in God, very interested in spirituality and very committed to wanting to change the world. Given the right space and the right conditions they will want to give voice to their longing for God and their longing for a better world. In the home, sometimes this will be best expressed by silence, by images, by listening to music, by meditative reading. And sometimes by discussion which then may lead into prayer.

With teenagers this might be something that happens once a week rather than every day.

"You gave your Son to share in the life of a family in Nazareth. Help us to value our families, to be thankful for them, and to live sensitively with them."

NEW PATTERNS FOR WORSHIP

Faith at home offers resources to help us discover God in the place we spend most of our time. It includes support for families in how to discuss faith and develop their practices and habits together. Find out more at
www.CofE.io/FaithAtHome

Teenagers can teach the rest of us a lot about prayer. They will want to live their prayer, and see prayer in action, or they will soon lose interest. They challenge the rest of us to see the connection between prayer and life.

———————————————

Thank you for the world so sweet;
Thank you for the food we eat;
Thank you for the birds that sing;
Thank you God for everything.
Amen.

EDITH RUTTER-LEATHAM

Question 6

Do I need words to pray?

Like so many things in life, so with prayer, going deeper often means less, not more.

Here are some ways of simplifying and purifying your prayer each day.

The simplest prayer of all is just saying the name of Jesus.

"All who call on the name of the Lord will be saved," says St Paul (Romans 10.3). The name Jesus means "God saves". As we say his name, so we invite Jesus to be with us.

The Jesus Prayer

This way of praying is known as the Jesus prayer. It is very popular in the Orthodox tradition of the church. There are various wordings, all roughly the same. One of the most common is:

Lord Jesus Christ, Son of the living God, have mercy on me, a sinner.

It's based on the cry of the repentant tax collector in Jesus' parable: "God, be merciful to me, a sinner" (Luke 18.13). But it also echoes St Paul's great hymn of praise in Philippians: Jesus is the Son of God but empties himself to take the form of a servant (Philippians 2.6-11).

Try saying the prayer over and over again. Breathe in on the first two phrases - *Lord Jesus Christ, Son of the living God.* And breathe out on the third - *have mercy on me a sinner.* As you do so, breathe in the righteousness and peace of God, and cast out all those things that separate us from God.

It is a prayer that is to be said slowly. It is meant to be said many times over. It is one of the simplest ways of praying. It can be prayed by anyone, anywhere.

If you find yourself sometimes waiting in the dark of the night and gripped by fear or anxiety, it is a wonderful way of calming the spirit.

This kind of prayer is also a good way of praying when we are feeling tired or distracted, or where we just don't know what to say.

Holding cross

And if even saying the name of Jesus becomes impossible - in the loneliness of isolation, anxiety or illness - another way of praying is to hold on to the cross of Christ.

I always carry a holding cross in my pocket. I often find myself clutching it and receiving comfort. It is a tangible reminder of the cross of Christ through which I have been brought into relationship with God.

When my father was dying, I gave him a holding cross. When he was no longer able to speak to me, he held onto the cross. When he died the cross was in his hand.

Silence

Then there is that prayer which has no words at all. "Be still and know that I am God," says the psalmist (Psalm 46.10).

The prayer which is stillness and silence is about waiting on God and letting God be God. The awesome majesty of God stops us in our tracks; silences the frantic jabber of our minds; and brings us to our knees. This kind of silence is not emptiness: it is heavy with the mighty presence of God. In all our prayers, and however we find prayer working for us, there should always be this silence and this waiting upon God.

Paradoxically, some of us find interior silence easier when we are moving. But this walk could be a prayer walk. We walk and reflect. We walk and we pray for others.

If you don't find silence easy, then begin with just a few moments. But as you grow in prayer, so you will also find that you grow in an ability to find this interior stillness.

The Lord's Prayer

Finally, the heart and foundation of all Christian prayer is the Lord's Prayer. If we do nothing else, we should try to recite this prayer at least once every day.

It is to this prayer, and what it can teach us about the whole of prayer, that we will turn next.

"*Be still, then, and know that I am God.*"

PSALM 46.11

Are there any other prayers you know by heart? You could try keeping a notebook of new prayers you discover.

The next time you're in a quiet place, listen to the silence …

———————————

Our Father in heaven,
hallowed be your name,
your kingdom come,
your will be done,
on earth as in heaven.
Give us today our daily bread.
Forgive us our sins
as we forgive those who sin against us.
Lead us not into temptation
but deliver us from evil.
For the kingdom, the power,
and the glory are yours
now and for ever.
Amen.

THE LORD'S PRAYER IN CONTEMPORARY LANGUAGE

Question 7

How did Jesus teach us to pray?

When the disciples asked Jesus to teach them how to pray, he gave them a simple formula. He said, "When you pray, this is what you say" (Luke 11.2).

He then told them that prayer that we know as the Lord's Prayer.

This is interesting. Jesus didn't exhort them to spend hours in meditation. Nor did he expect them to always be able to express prayer in their own words. Of course, he longed that they would grow in the same intimate relationship with God that we see in his own life and ministry. But his first priority was to give them a prayer that would be the foundation and the heart of all prayer.

So, the Lord's Prayer teaches us all we need to know about prayer.

Here is a short and simple way of beginning to understand this.

Our Father in heaven

To say *Our Father* means to recognise that the heart of prayer is relationship with God. God is like a loving parent. When we pray we come into relationship with the one who loves us unconditionally. Even if other human relationships, even our own parents, have let us down, God will not.

Also, God is not "my father", but "our father". The Lord's Prayer doesn't just bring us into relationship with God, it brings us into relationship with each other. By saying this prayer, we acknowledge our solidarity with all those who are our sisters and brothers.

Hallowed be your name

To say *hallowed be your name* means that we give God thanks and praise, acknowledging our dependence on God. We recognise that God is the source of everything and that nothing exists - not even the next breath we are about to take - without God.

We adore God, not because God needs adoration, but because God has shown us his love in Jesus Christ and brought us into this living relationship.

Your kingdom come, your will be done

To say *your kingdom come, your will be done*, means that we surrender our will to God's will. We seek God's purposes for God's world.

Some people imagine that somehow praying might change God's mind on something. It's as if they're thinking: if we could just get enough signatures on the prayer petition, maybe God would change his mind. But the purpose of prayer is not that we might change God's mind, but that God might change ours.

On earth as in heaven

We seek God's kingdom - that is God's reign of justice and peace - *on earth as in heaven*. We seek to align our will with the will of God. Even Jesus had to learn this in his earthly life and ministry. We see this when he battled with the devil in the wilderness. We see it most poignantly in the garden of Gethsemane when he prayed that, if it were possible, God might take the cup away from him. But after much struggle and anguish, Jesus arrives at a point where he can completely accept and receive God's will for his life.

Give us today our daily bread

To pray *give us today our daily bread* means asking God to show us what "enough" looks like. We ask God to give us today what we need for today and to save us from craving more than our share. This goes against the grain of the way we usually live our lives.

Forgive us our sins as we forgive those who sin against us

If we come to God with penitent hearts, being honest about our failings and our need of God's grace, God is always ready to forgive. When we say *forgive us our sins as we forgive those who sin against us* we are acknowledging our need of God, and we are asking God not just to be merciful to us, but to enable us to be merciful to others.

We have all had the experience of going to bed and thinking "why did I say that?", or "why did I do the other?" When this happens, we are recognising our sinfulness even if we don't actually use the word. We are acknowledging that we fall short of our own standards. However, even reflecting very briefly on the life and teaching of Jesus, shows us that we also fall short of God's standards.

This is the reality of sin. We are not the people we are meant to be. We are not even the people we want to be. We are certainly not the people God intended us to be. But God, who is loving and merciful, the lover who comes into our presence to tell us we are loved, is always ready to forgive.

Lead us not into temptation but deliver us from evil

When we say *lead us not into temptation but deliver us from evil* we are acknowledging both our human frailty and our human destiny. One day we will all die. At that point - the time of trial - we are asking God to deliver us from the snares of evil, from the terrible temptation to still put self first, and to bring us, through Jesus, into everlasting life.

For the kingdom, the power, and the glory are yours now and for ever and ever

So the Lord's Prayer ends with this final affirmation of God's sovereignty over all things and for all time.

Amen

This word – the word that ends all prayers – means "I agree". Or "so be it". It is a way of giving our own affirmation and seal of approval and commitment to the words we say. This is especially important for the Lord's Prayer. It is a radically beautiful and life-changing prayer.

We should say it as if we mean it. We should expect it to change us.

Don't say *Amen* at the end unless you are ready for such a revolution!

"We do not complain
of what God
does not give us;
rather we thank God
for what he does
give us daily."

DIETRICH BONHOEFFER

What does it mean that God rules over everything? How might this affect your life?

When might you pray the Lord's Prayer tomorrow?

----

*Lord of heaven and earth,
as Jesus taught his disciples
to be persistent in prayer,
give us patience and courage
never to lose hope,
but always to bring
our prayers before you;
through Jesus Christ our Lord.
Amen.*

COMMON WORSHIP RITES ON THE WAY

Question 8

How do I pray when prayer seems impossible?

Throughout Christian history, when people sought to deepen their relationship with God they went into the desert. They pursued isolation. This way of living the Christian vocation was called the solitary life.

Abba Moses, one of the Desert Fathers, used to say to his novices, "Go to your cell, and your cell will teach you everything."

Those early monks who fled into the desert were imitating Jesus in his isolation. There are many times in the gospels where Jesus deliberately removes himself from people. He disappears off to a deserted place to pray (Mark 1.32). He dismisses the crowds and goes up a mountain on his own (Matthew 14.23). He sits by a well in the desert (John 4.5). He prays on his own on the night before his death (Luke 22.41). In particular, the monks remembered the days Jesus spent in the wilderness and the temptations he faced there (Matthew 4.1-11).

Encountering the darkness

The spiritual life always involves an encounter with darkness. The people of Israel are led through the desert into the Promised Land. Jesus began his ministry being driven into the wilderness. The garden of the resurrection is entered through his suffering on Calvary. Similarly, our faith must pass through periods of barren difficulty, doubt and despair.

But doubt is not the opposite of faith. The opposite of doubt is certainty. Doubting is part of believing. It is the shadow that is created by the light. This is why when people become Christians, we do not ask them to say that they know beyond doubt that Jesus is the one they must follow. We ask them if they believe and trust.

When we follow Christ we are not giving our assent to a set of abstract propositions, but to a person. To the living God who is made known to us as Father, Son and Holy Spirit. We are saying that God is community, and that we are called to live our lives in community with God and with each other.

It is often in prayer that we become most aware of the dark and difficult times of the Christian journey.

Sometimes this is because we are facing a crisis or a tragedy in our life or in the life of the world. Sometimes it can be what feels like a loss of faith. We feel angry and resentful towards God. It feels as if God has let us down, or even abandoned us. Prayer suddenly feels impossible or useless. God seems absent.

When this happens prayer becomes empty, familiar words and rituals lose their comfort. Church becomes boring. Other Christians become irritating, and faith can suddenly feel a ridiculous charade. The energy of our faith is sapped.

Although these experiences are dark and terrible, they are also normal and inevitable. All the great spiritual writers speak of the desert experience as part of the Christian journey.

Many Christians are ill-prepared for the dark times that will inevitably come. Often people not only give up on prayer, but give up on God when they find themselves in the desert.

You might be feeling great despair and darkness right now. Prayer might have become very difficult. But if all you do is hold on to your desire to pray, then you are already on the road to recovery.

Finding refreshment in the desert

When you journey through the desert, what you look for is an oasis: a place where you can quench your thirst. The oasis will be different for each of us: it might be a familiar prayer; a verse from scripture; a piece of music; a photograph; or even some symbolic action. Discern what it is - no matter how small and seemingly insignificant - that still connects you to God, and hold onto it tightly through the desert.

Discern what it is that still connects you to God, and hold onto it tightly.

Some of the things you have read about here can be your oasis in this desert. Even if it is just clutching the holding cross in your pocket. Or crying out the name of Jesus from the depths of sadness and fear, then you are a person of prayer, in community with God and held by Jesus. As you hold onto him and cry out to him, he is holding you.

In the Bible, the desert is always a place of discovery. The prophet Isaiah says, "The wilderness and the dry land shall be glad, the desert shall rejoice and blossom." (Isaiah 35.1)

May this be true for you, too.

"If I say, 'Surely the darkness shall cover me, and the light around me become night', even the darkness is not dark to you; the night is as bright as the day, for darkness is as light to you."

PSALM 139.11–12

Do you know Psalm 23, "The Lord is my shepherd", which is itself a beautiful prayer? Find a copy of the text, and next time you are feeling sad, read from it.

Could you commit to memory a prayer that will stay with you even (maybe especially) when you feel far from God?

---

*O Lord, support us all the day long
of this troublous life,
until the shadows lengthen,
and the evening comes,
and the busy world is hushed,
and the fever of life is over,
and our work is done.
Then, Lord, in thy mercy
grant us a safe lodging,
a holy rest, and peace at the last;
through Jesus Christ our Lord.
Amen.*

JOHN HENRY NEWMAN

Question 9

How do I go deeper in prayer?

Reading the Bible each day is a basic part of the Christian diet. Other spiritual books, apps and podcasts can also be very helpful. I've tried to signpost just a few resources here that might help you take the next step in your prayer journey.

Reflective Bible reading

This way of reading the Bible reflectively is traditionally known as Lectio Divina ("holy reading"). It dates back to the early centuries of the Christian Church and St Benedict encouraged its use in monasteries in the sixth century. It is a way of praying the Scriptures that leads us deeper into God's word. We slow down. We read a short passage more than once. We chew it over slowly and carefully. We savour it. Scripture begins to speak to us in a new way. It speaks to us personally, and aids that union we have with God through Christ who is himself the Living Word.

You can do it on your own; with those who share your home, or in a group or a conference call with others.

A prayer before Bible reading

O Lord, you have given us your word
for a light to shine upon our path.
Grant us so to meditate on that word,
and to follow its teaching,
that we may find in it the light
that shines more and more
until the perfect day;
through Jesus Christ our Lord. Amen.

A PRAYER BEFORE BIBLE READING, AFTER JEROME (420)

The Psalms

The psalms have always had a very significant place in Christian prayer. In today's church they are not as familiar as they used to be, though many churches and cathedrals still say or sing the psalms as a regular part of their worship. Perhaps now is the time to renew our acquaintance with the "prayer book of the Bible"?

The psalms give us words to express our joy, our faithfulness, our frustration, and our fear.

The Psalms are a tremendous resource for our praying, especially when we're not sure what to say. This is the reason they endure. The psalms give us words to express our joy, our faithfulness, our frustration, and our fear. Whatever you are feeling about almost any given situation, there is a psalm that will match it and trump it. So, if you are feeling joyful, there is a psalm that is more joyful than you. If you are feeling alienated or alone, there is a psalm that is more isolated than you. At our time of need we have words at hand. And at the same time these same words extend and enlarge our faith.

Jesus died with the words of the psalms on his lips and in his heart. The words that he had learned in his youth sustained him. For Christians, some of these psalms – especially Psalm 22 and Psalm 69 – become profound mediations on Christ's passion and death. When we face suffering, perhaps the illness or death of a loved one, then these are words that we can turn to.

Jesus obviously knew at least some of the psalms by heart. Ours is an age where some of the spiritual and disciplines which helped to form our forebears as Christians have fallen into disuse. So, for instance, the idea of reading prayers and learning things by heart is out of fashion.

Here is a last little challenge: why not learn a psalm by heart – perhaps Psalm 23, that most comforting of psalms suggested at the end of the previous section? If you do this, you will be giving yourself a gift that will last lifetime, a prayer that you can draw on in your hour of need.

Prayer beads

This ancient way of praying uses knotted string or beads. The prayer is rhythmic. As we pass each knot or bead through our fingers, we say short prayers that have been committed to memory.

The most famous of these forms of prayer is called the rosary. As a set pattern of prayers is recited, the person praying meditates on different aspects of the Christian story. You can find the set prayers online if you would like to explore this way of praying. Once you have got into the rhythm of the prayer, you can concentrate on the story of the gospel as you recite the prayers.

Prayer beads and prayers string can be great for children.

Prayer beads and prayer strings can be great for children. They will enjoy making them as well as using them. You can either follow a set pattern, like the rosary, or make up your own patterns.

"Don't make your prayer life depend on the whims of the moment; make it a regular, daily practice. God is always present, always loving, and he is waiting for you."

MICHAEL QUOIST,
THE CHRISTIAN RESPONSE

There are plenty of books that you can read about prayer. Much of the material here is adapted from my own longer book *How to Pray: alone, with others, at any time, in any place*, which includes a list of further resources.

The Pilgrim Course *is shaped around reflective reading of the Bible.* A good place to start is the course on *The Lord's Prayer*. There are sample sessions – and free audio and video resources – available to download via **www.pilgrimcourse.org**

The Church of England's Daily Prayer *app* offers a daily diet of psalms and Bible readings, and the accompanying *Reflections for Daily Prayer* app, book or eBook makes a good companion, with a short meditation on one of the passages set for each day. Find out more at **www.dailyprayer.org.uk**

Other popular apps to help with daily Bible reading and reflection include **Pray As You Go** and **Lectio 365**.

Question 10

Now I've started praying, how do I keep going?

When we pray, we are not putting money in the heavenly slot machine to get what we want or to make a transaction with God. Prayer isn't just asking for things.

Question 10

We can and do ask for things. What could be more natural than to come to the one we love with the requests and concerns of our hearts?

But more than asking for what we want, prayer is receiving from God what God wants to give us. When we pray, we are resting in the presence of the one who loves us and who knows what is best for us.

This is why we keep going with prayer, even when it is hard. We don't give up on the ones we love. To know God and to know that we are loved by God is the only reward we need.

Many people find prayer difficult because they have a picture in their mind of what it is supposed to be like. Then they feel a failure if their prayers don't match up. Sitting in blissful silence for half an hour, your mind empty of everything but God? A wildly joyful and ecstatic experience in which you speak in tongues of Pentecostal fire? Or eloquently bringing before God the needs of everyone and everything in the world? If you imagine that prayer will always be like one of these, then you probably won't get very far.

But prayer is relationship with God. So, like every other relationship, it is nurtured in small acts of attentive kindness. In the best and most intimate relationships sometimes it's just enough to be in the presence of the one you love. You don't necessarily have to do or say anything. But small words and gestures of love will always help.

Knowing God is not the only way to be happy in life. There are many happy and fulfilled people in the world who are not Christians. But the fullness that we long for only comes from God, because everything which is good and fulfilling ultimately comes from God. And nothing which is good is outside the heart of God. So, when we seek the heart of God in prayer, we are seeking the deepest joy of all and the deepest fulfilment. When we pray, we come to the peak of the mountain in whose foothills we have always wandered.

More than asking for what we want, prayer is receiving from God what God wants to give us.

Also, the results, such as they are, are most likely to be seen by others, not us. As St Paul says, as we see the glory of the Lord as though reflected in a mirror, so we "are being transformed into the same image from one degree of glory to another" (1 Corinthians 3.18).

Making your life a prayer

When we start to live this way - knowing we are loved by God, being secure in that love, and bringing everything to God - then we find that the whole of life becomes a prayer, an offering of praise to God. This life is nurtured and watered by regular times of prayer. But slowly - and over the course of a lifetime it changes everything. Even the world.

_____

When we start to live this way ... we find that the whole of life becomes a prayer.

_____

Someone once asked me how long this takes? I was able to give them a precise answer. It takes a lifetime. By happy coincidence that is exactly how much time each one of us has been given.

One lifetime to live in praise of God and to be part of God's mission of love to the world.

"Your prayer will take
countless forms …
Sometimes you will taste and see
how good the Lord is …
Sometimes you will be
dry and joyless …
Sometimes you will be able
to do nothing else
but take your whole life
and everything in you
and bring them before God.
Every hour has its own possibilities
of genuine prayer.
So set yourself again and again
on the way of prayer."

RULE FOR A NEW BROTHER

Go back through this material and highlight parts that call out to you. Think about how you could act on one of them today.

If you've found this helpful, who do you know who would benefit from reading this? Find a way to share it with them.

---

*Almighty God,
in Christ you make all things new:
transform the poverty of our nature
by the riches of your grace,
and in the renewal of our lives
make known your heavenly glory;
through Jesus Christ
your Son our Lord,
who is alive and reigns with you,
in the unity of the Holy Spirit,
one God, now and for ever. Amen.*

THE COLLECT FOR THE SECOND SUNDAY
OF EPIPHANY, COMMON WORSHIP

Sources

St Augustine of Hippo, *Confessions*, trans. F. K. Sheed, Sheed and Ward, 1942.

Dietrich Bonhoeffer, *Letters and Papers from Prison*, enlarged edition, SCM Press, 1971.

Common Worship: Services and Prayers for the Church of England, Church House Publishing, 2000.

Common Worship: Daily Prayer, Church House Publishing, 2005.

Common Worship: Rites on the Way, 2006.

Ken Leech, *Soul Friend*, Sheldon Press, 1977.

Thomas Merton, *The Wisdom of the Desert*, Sheldon Press, 1973.

Julian of Norwich, *Revelations of Divine Love*, Penguin Books, 1966.

New Patterns for Worship, Church House Publishing, 2002.

Henri Nouwen, *Seeds of Hope*, Darton, Longman and Todd, 1989.

Elizabeth Ruth Obbard, *To Live is to Pray: An Introduction to Carmelite Spirituality*, Canterbury Press, 1997.

Michel Quoist, *The Christian Response*, Gill and Macmillan, 1965.

Rule for a New Brother, Darton, Longman and Todd, 1973.

Mother Teresa of Calcutta, *In the Silence of the Heart*, SPCK, 1983.